JANICE MURFITT

MEREHURST

LONDON

Contents

Managing Editor: Janet Illsley
Photographer: Alan Newnham
Designer: Sue Storey
Food Stylist: Janice Murfitt
Photographic Stylist: Maria Jacques
Typeset by Angel Graphics
Colour separation by J. Film Process Limited, Thailand
Printed in Italy by New Interlitho S.p.A.

First published 1990 by Merehurst Ltd,
Ferry House, 51/57 Lacy Road, Putney, London SW15 1PR
Reprinted 1991

© Merehurst Ltd

ISBN: 1 85391 132 1 (Cased)
ISBN: 1 85391 215 8 (Paperback)

NOTES
All spoon measures are level: 1 tablespoon = 15ml spoon;
1 teaspoon = 5ml spoon.
Use greaseproof paper for lining cake tins unless otherwise stated.

Introduction

I have always enjoyed making cakes. I often hear people say 'you can either make cakes or you can't' but there are no real secrets to this art, just a few simple guidelines.

To obtain a cake with a good texture, flavour and depth, a fine balance of ingredients is essential. It is therefore important to measure accurately and keep to the ingredients and quantities stated. Make sure your cake tin is the correct shape and size, too; remember a square tin is larger than a similar round one.

Ovens vary greatly – some being hot, others too cool. Check your oven with a thermometer if possible and adjust settings if necessary. Test cakes just before the stated cooking time, and always before removing from the oven.

Cakes must be kept in a cool place – in a tin, or wrapped in foil or plastic wrap. Plastic containers are not ideal, they are vacuum sealed and are inclined to promote mould growth – especially at room temperature. All cakes made with dried fruit which have a simple glazed topping will keep for several weeks. Those which include fresh fruit in the cake or topping must be stored in a very cool place or in the refrigerator and eaten within 4-5 days. Gâteaux and cakes with a fresh cream topping must similarly be kept very cool and consumed within 1-2 days.

In this book, you will find a cake for every occasion – from quick simple cakes made with wholesome fruits, nuts and cereals – to elaborate gâteaux. Soft, light sponges enclose unusual fillings, featuring natural ingredients and fresh fruits. These delicious cakes are coated with a variety of frostings and icings. All of the recipes included are easy to follow, with suggested variations. I hope you will find them a source of inspiration.

3

Summer Lemon Cake

A light lemon sponge – kept moist by a lemon crème au beurre icing. Try replacing the lemons with oranges or limes.

3 eggs
90g (3oz/⅓ cup) caster sugar
60g (2oz/½ cup) plain flour
30g (1oz/3 tablespoons)
  cornflour
30g (1oz) unsalted
  butter, melted
2 teaspoons grated lemon rind

CREME AU BEURRE:
90g (3oz/⅓ cup) caster sugar
4 tablespoons lemon juice
2 egg yolks
155g (5oz) unsalted butter,
  softened
TO DECORATE:
lemon rind shreds

1 Lightly grease and line a 20cm (8 inch) round cake tin. Preheat oven to 180C (350F/Gas 4).

2 Place eggs and sugar in a heatproof bowl over a saucepan of simmering water. Whisk until the mixture becomes thick and pale. Remove bowl from pan and whisk until the mixture leaves a trail on the surface when the beaters are lifted.

3 Sift the flour and cornflour onto the surface of the mixture; add butter and lemon rind. Carefully fold into mixture using a spatula until all flour is incorporated. Pour mixture into prepared tin and bake in oven for 35-40 minutes, or until the cake springs back when pressed in the centre. Turn out onto a wire rack to cool.

4 To make crème au beurre, place sugar and lemon juice in a saucepan and heat gently until sugar has dissolved, then boil rapidly for 1-2 minutes to thread stage (when a little of the mixture placed between the backs of 2 teaspoons and pulled apart forms a thread). Pour syrup in a steady stream onto egg yolks, whisking all the time. Continue whisking until mixture is thick and pale. Beat butter until light and fluffy, then gradually beat in egg mixture, until thick.

5 Cut cake into 2 layers. Sandwich together with lemon icing and cover top and sides with more icing. Pipe a border around the edge. Decorate with lemon shreds. *Serves 12.*

Chocolate Fudge Cake

A scrumptious chocolate cake – everyone's favourite! I have included ground almonds to give a moist, soft texture and covered the cake with a rich chocolate frosting.

125g (4oz/1 cup) self-raising
flour
3 tablespoons cocoa powder
60g (2oz/¹/₂ cup) ground
almonds
155g (5oz/²/₃ cup) caster sugar
125ml (4 fl oz/¹/₂ cup)
sunflower oil
3 eggs, separated
125ml (4 fl oz/¹/₂ cup)
boiling water

CHOCOLATE FUDGE ICING:
125g (4oz) plain (dark)
chocolate, in pieces
60g (2oz) unsalted butter
1 egg, beaten
185g (6oz/1 cup) icing sugar,
sifted
TO DECORATE:
24 split almonds
6 mimosa balls

1 Lightly grease and base line two 20cm (8 inch) round sandwich tins. Preheat oven to 160C (325F/Gas 3).
2 Sift flour and cocoa powder together into a bowl. Stir in ground almonds and caster sugar; make a well in centre. Whisk oil and egg yolks together in a jug, then add to dry ingredients with boiling water. Beat to a smooth batter. Stiffly whisk egg whites, add to chocolate mixture and fold in carefully using a spatula.
3 Divide mixture evenly between prepared tins, smooth tops and bake in oven for 20-25 minutes, or until cakes spring back when lightly pressed in the centre. Turn out onto a wire rack to cool.
4 To make chocolate fudge icing, melt chocolate and butter in a bowl over a saucepan of hot water. Stir in egg, then add icing sugar and beat until smooth.
5 Sandwich cakes together with a quarter of the icing. Place cake on wire rack over a plate and pour remaining icing over to cover completely. Leave to set. Spoon icing from plate into a piping bag fitted with a star nozzle and pipe 8 swirls around top edge of cake. Decorate with almonds and mimosa. *Serves 12.*

Passion Cake

Passion fruit with its intensely flavoured flesh and edible seeds gives this cake its distinctive flavour and unusual texture. If you prefer a smooth texture simply use the juice and discard the seeds.

185g (6oz/1½ cups) self-raising flour
1½ teaspoons baking powder
185g (6oz/¾ cup) caster sugar
185g (6oz) soft margarine
3 eggs, beaten
2 passion fruit

PASSION FRUIT FROSTING:
3 passion fruit
60g (2oz) soft margarine
250g (8oz/1½ cups) icing sugar, sifted
TO FINISH:
cocoa powder for dusting

1 Lightly grease and line a 20cm (8 inch) square cake tin. Preheat oven to 160C (325F/Gas 3).

2 Sift flour and baking powder into a mixing bowl, then add sugar, margarine and eggs. Mix with a wooden spoon, then beat for 1-2 minutes until smooth and glossy. Cut passion fruit in half, scoop out flesh and seeds and add to cake mixture; stir until well blended.

3 Place mixture in prepared tin, smooth top and bake in oven for 40-45 minutes, or until cake springs back when lightly pressed in centre. Cool in tin for 5 minutes, turn out onto a wire rack, remove paper and turn cake right way up. Leave until cold.

4 To make passion fruit frosting, halve passion fruit, scoop out flesh and seeds into a nylon sieve over a bowl and press out juice using a wooden spoon. Add margarine to bowl and place over a saucepan of simmering water until melted. Add icing sugar and beat until mixture is smooth and glossy.

5 Place cake on a wire rack over a plate, pour frosting over to cover completely and leave to set. Cut out 12 strips of paper 23 x 1cm (9 x ½ inch) and arrange on cake in a lattice. Sift cocoa over top of cake, then carefully remove each strip leaving a neat pattern. *Serves 18-24.*

Pineapple Balmoral Cake

A refreshing cake flavoured with the tang of fresh pineapple. Use canned pineapple as a standby.

1 small pineapple
125g (4oz) butter, softened
125g (4oz/½ cup) caster sugar
2 eggs, beaten
155g (5oz/1¼ cups) self-raising flour
30g (1oz/3 tablespoons) cornflour

1 teaspoon baking powder
PINEAPPLE FROSTING:
120ml (4 fl oz/½ cup) pineapple (see below)
250g (8oz/1½ cups) icing sugar, sifted
TO DECORATE:
pineapple slices (see below)

1 Cut 3 thin slices from the pineapple and reserve for decoration. Peel remaining pineapple and cut out hard centre core. Finely chop 125g (4oz) pineapple. Purée the remaining pineapple in a blender or food processor; reserve for the frosting.

2 Grease and lightly flour a 30 x 10cm (12 x 4in) Balmoral cake tin. Preheat oven to 160C (325F/Gas 3). Beat butter and sugar together in a bowl until light and fluffy. Gradually add eggs, beating well after each addition. Sift flour, cornflour and baking powder over mixture and fold in carefully using a spatula until all flour is incorporated. Fold in chopped pineapple.

3 Place mixture in prepared tin, smooth top and bake for 55-60 minutes, or until cake springs back when pressed in the centre. Leave cake in tin for 5 minutes, then turn out onto a wire rack and leave until cold.

4 To make pineapple frosting, measure 120ml (4 fl oz/ ½ cup) pineapple purée and place in a bowl. Stir in icing sugar and beat until smooth. Pour frosting evenly over cake. Cut reserved pineapple slices into wedges and arrange on top of cake. Leave to set. *Serves 14-18.*

NOTE: If you do not have a Balmoral cake tin, you can use a 1kg (2lb) loaf tin and allow an extra 10-15 minutes cooking.

Sticky Ginger Cake

A really moist cake with good keeping qualities, topped with a tangy orange butter icing. For a spice cake, replace ginger with mixed spice and flavour the icing with lemon or lime.

125g (4oz/4 tablespoons)
  golden syrup
125g (4oz/4 tablespoons)
  black treacle
140ml (4½ fl oz/7 tablespoons)
  sunflower oil
125g (4oz/¾ cup) light soft
  brown sugar
125ml (4 fl oz/½ cup) milk
250g (8oz/2 cups) plain flour
3 teaspoons ground ginger
1 egg, beaten

½ teaspoon bicarbonate of soda
ORANGE BUTTER ICING:
90g (3oz) unsalted butter,
  softened
3 teaspoons finely grated
  orange rind
4 teaspoons orange juice
185g (6oz/1 cup) icing sugar,
  sifted
TO DECORATE:
3 pieces crystallized ginger,
  thinly sliced

1 Lightly grease and line a 20cm (8in) square cake tin. Preheat oven to 150C (300F/Gas 2).

2 Measure golden syrup, treacle and oil carefully into a saucepan. Add brown sugar and milk and place over a low heat, stirring occasionally, until melted.

3 Sift flour and ginger into a bowl and add egg. Remove pan from heat, stir in bicarbonate of soda and quickly pour onto flour mixture. Using a wooden spoon, beat until smooth.

4 Pour mixture into prepared tin and bake for 60-70 minutes or until cake springs back when pressed in centre. Leave in tin for 5 minutes, then turn out onto a wire rack, remove paper, turn cake right way up and leave until cold.

5 To make orange butter icing, put butter into a bowl and beat with a wooden spoon until soft. Add orange rind, juice and icing sugar and beat together until light and fluffy.

6 Spread two thirds of the icing evenly over top of cake, marking icing with lines. Place remaining icing in a piping bag fitted with a small star nozzle and pipe a border around edge of cake. Decorate with crystallized ginger. *Serves 20.*

Kumquat Ring

Tiny flavoursome kumquats combine the flavour of orange with the tang of lemons, imparting a refreshing flavour to this whole-wheat sponge.

175g (6oz/1½ cups) self-raising
*   wholemeal flour*
1½ teaspoons baking powder
175g (6oz/1 cup) light soft
*   brown sugar*
175g (6oz) soft margarine
3 eggs

6 kumquats, thinly sliced
TOPPING:
90g (3oz/⅓ cup) caster sugar
125ml (4 fl oz/½ cup) water
10 kumquats, thinly sliced
15-18 angelica diamonds

1 Lightly grease a 23cm (9 inch) ring tin. Preheat oven to 160C (325F/Gas 3).

2 Sift flour and baking powder into a mixing bowl, then add sugar, margarine and eggs. Mix together with a wooden spoon, then beat for 1-2 minutes until smooth and glossy. Stir in kumquats.

3 Spoon mixture into prepared tin and smooth the top. Bake in oven for 35-40 minutes, or until cake springs back when lightly pressed in the centre. Loosen edges with palette knife, turn cake out onto a wire rack and leave until cold.

4 For the topping, place sugar and water in a small saucepan and heat gently until melted, stirring occasionally. Add kumquat slices and cook for 1 minute until tender. Lift out using a slotted spoon and arrange kumquat slices overlapping around top of ring cake. Position angelica pieces in between.

5 Boil remaining syrup for 1 minute until the syrup reaches the thread stage. To test, press a small amount of syrup between the backs of 2 teaspoons: when pulled apart a thread should form. Pour syrup evenly over kumquat topping to glaze. *Serves 10.*

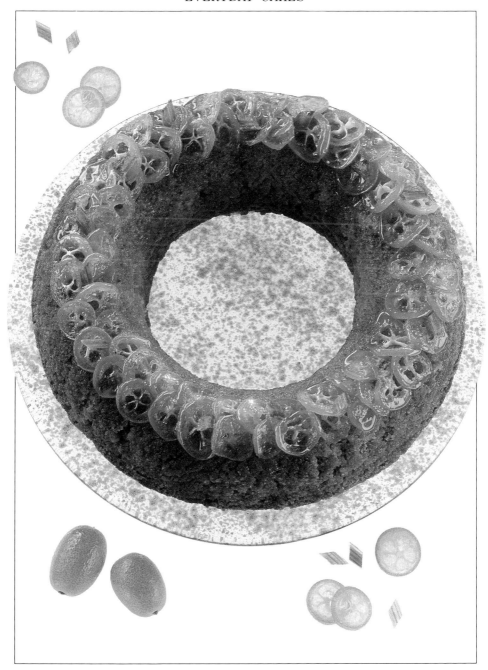

Creamy Apricot Roll

A naturally healthy filling of dried apricots blended with low fat soft cheese gives a fresh, fruity contrast to this light sponge roll. For a different flavour, try dried apples or peaches.

SWISS ROLL:
3 eggs
90g (3oz/1/3 cup) caster sugar
90g (3oz/3/4 cup) plain flour
APRICOT FILLING:
125g (4oz/1 cup) pre-soaked dried apricots

185ml (6 fl oz/3/4 cup) orange juice
185g (6oz/3/4 cup) soft cheese
TO DECORATE:
icing sugar for dusting
6 apricots, halved

1 First make apricot filling: place apricots and orange juice in a saucepan, bring to the boil, cover and cook gently until nearly all the juice is absorbed. Purée in a blender or food processor, then leave until cold. Place a third of the soft cheese in a piping bag fitted with a star nozzle and set aside. Beat remainder into apricot purée.

2 Lightly grease and line a 33 x 23cm (13 x 9in) Swiss roll tin. Preheat oven to 180C (350F/Gas 4).

3 Place eggs and sugar in a heatproof bowl over a pan of simmering water and whisk until thick and pale. Remove bowl from saucepan and whisk until mixture leaves a trail on the surface when beaters are lifted.

4 Sift flour onto surface of mixture and carefully fold in using a spatula until all flour is incorporated. Pour mixture into prepared tin and tilt tin from side to side to level surface. Bake in oven for 10-15 minutes or until cake springs back when pressed in centre.

5 Turn cake out onto a piece of greaseproof paper dusted with icing sugar. Peel off lining paper, trim off edges and spread evenly with apricot mixture. Roll up sponge from the short edge. Cool on a wire rack. When cold, pipe with soft cheese and decorate with apricot halves. *Serves 10.*

Cherry Topped Madeira

A good homely cherry madeira cake, with ground almonds added to keep the cake moist. Top with red and yellow glacé cherries and glacé fruits, or mixed dried fruits.

185g (6oz) butter, softened
185g (6oz/³/4 cup) caster sugar
3 eggs, beaten
185g (6oz/1¹/2 cups) self-raising flour
60g (2oz/¹/2 cup) ground almonds
155g (4oz/³/4 cup) glacé cherries, finely chopped

TO GLAZE:
2 tablespoons apricot jam
2 teaspoons water
60g (2oz/¹/3 cup) glacé cherries, halved
3 glacé pineapple rings, cut into pieces

1 Lightly grease and line an 18cm (7 inch) round cake tin. Preheat oven to 160C (325F/Gas 3).

2 Beat butter and sugar together in a bowl until light and fluffy. Gradually add eggs, beating well after each addition. Sift in flour, add ground almonds and chopped cherries and fold carefully into mixture using a spatula.

3 Place mixture in prepared tin, smooth top and bake for 1 hour–1¹/4 hours or until cake springs back when pressed in the centre. Cool in tin for 5 minutes, turn out onto a wire rack, remove paper, invert cake and leave until cold.

4 For the glaze, place apricot jam and water in a small saucepan and bring to the boil, stirring occasionally. Sieve and brush over top of cake. Arrange halved glacé cherries and pineapple pieces on top and brush with remaining glaze. Leave to set. *Serves 12.*

Spiced Apple Cake

When apples are plentiful, combine them with a mixture of spices to make this delicious moist cake. Decorate with red and green apple slices for a tempting top. Pears or plums can be used in place of the apples. Store in a cool place and eat within 2-3 days, or omit the topping and simply glaze with honey to store for up to a week.

250g (8oz) peeled and cored
   apples, grated
155g (5oz) soft margarine
185g (6oz/¾ cup) caster sugar
60g (2oz/⅓ cup) currants
60g (2oz/½ cup) pine nuts
2 eggs, beaten
280g (9oz/2¼ cups) plain flour
1 teaspoon bicarbonate of soda

1 teaspoon ground cinnamon
1 teaspoon ground nutmeg
½ teaspoon ground cloves
TOPPING:
1 red apple
1 green apple
1 tablespoon lemon juice
2 tablespoons icing sugar, sifted

1 Lightly grease an 18cm (7 inch) square cake tin. Preheat oven to 180C (350F/Gas 4).

2 Place the grated apple in a large mixing bowl with the margarine, sugar, currants, pine nuts and egg. Sift in flour, bicarbonate of soda and spices and mix together with a wooden spoon. Beat for 1-2 minutes until smooth and glossy.

3 Spoon mixture into prepared tin, smooth top and bake in oven for 1 hour 5 minutes to 1 hour 10 minutes, or until cake springs back when lightly pressed in centre. Leave in tin for 5 minutes, then turn out onto a wire rack, remove paper and allow to cool.

4 For the topping, cut apples into quarters, remove cores and slice thinly. Toss in lemon juice to prevent discolouring. Arrange apple slices over top of cake, dredge with icing sugar and place under a preheated hot grill for 1-2 minutes until sugar has caramelized. Leave to cool before serving.
Serves 18.

Carrot Cake

A really quick and easy recipe for a deliciously moist cake containing carrots, spices, raisins and honey. To vary the flavour, try cinnamon, nutmeg or mace instead of mixed spice; for a darker cake replace half of the honey with black treacle.

250g (8oz) carrots, finely grated
125g (4oz/³/₄ cup) raisins
60g (2oz/¹/₃ cup) figs, chopped
125g (4oz/¹/₂ cup) caster sugar
125g (4oz) unsalted butter
185g (6oz/¹/₂ cup) clear honey
155ml (5 fl oz/²/₃ cup) orange
* juice*
250g (8oz/2 cups) self-raising
* flour*

1 teaspoon ground mixed spice
1 egg, beaten
TOPPING:
185g (6oz/1 cup) icing sugar,
* sifted*
3 teaspoons orange juice
3 teaspoons grated orange rind
60g (2oz) marzipan
few drops of orange
* food colouring*

1 Lightly grease and base line a 23cm (9 inch) spring form cake tin. Preheat oven to 160C (325F/Gas 3).
2 Put carrots, raisins, figs, caster sugar, butter, honey and orange juice in a saucepan. Heat gently, stirring occasionally, until sugar and butter have melted. Transfer to a mixing bowl and allow to cool. Sift flour and spice together over mixture, add egg and beat thoroughly until well blended.
3 Place mixture in prepared tin, smooth top and bake in oven for 1 hour to 1 hour 10 minutes, or until cake springs back when lightly pressed in the centre. Loosen edge with a palette knife, unclip spring to release cake and remove base and paper. Cool on a wire rack.
4 To make the topping, combine the icing sugar and orange juice and beat until smooth. Spread icing evenly over top of cold cake. Knead orange rind and orange colouring into marzipan. Grate on a coarse grater and sprinkle around top edge of cake. Leave to set. *Serves 16.*

Apricot & Fig Corn Bread

This is one of those recipes where any mixture of dried fruits could be used: dates, prunes, apples and figs all blend well with the cornmeal mixture. Serve cut into slices and spread with butter.

125g (4oz/1 cup) pre-soaked
  dried apricots, chopped
90g (3oz/½ cup) dried figs,
  chopped
90g (3oz/½ cup) raisins
185ml (6 fl oz/¾ cup) apricot
  nectar
60g (2oz/⅓ cup) light soft brown
  sugar
1 egg, beaten

155g (5oz/1¼ cups) self-raising
  wholemeal flour
90g (3oz/⅔ cup) cornmeal
1 teaspoon baking powder
TOPPING:
2 tablespoons apricot jam,
  boiled and sieved
2 dried apricots, sliced
2 dried figs, sliced

1 Lightly grease and line a 500g (1lb) loaf tin. Preheat oven to 160C (325F/Gas 3).

2 Put apricots, figs and raisins into a mixing bowl. Heat apricot nectar and sugar in a small saucepan, pour onto fruit and stir well. Cover bowl with cling film and leave until cold.

3 Stir in egg, flour, cornmeal and baking powder. Using a wooden spoon, beat until well blended. Turn mixture into prepared tin, smooth top and bake in oven for 1 hour, or until cake springs back when lightly pressed in the centre.

4 Leave in tin for 5 minutes, then turn out onto a wire rack, remove paper, invert cake and leave until cold. Brush top with apricot jam to glaze. Decorate with apricots and figs and brush fruit with more glaze. *Serves 12.*

Courgette (Zucchini) Cake

When courgettes (zucchini) are plentiful, this is a good way to use them. This unusual cake, which includes mixed dried fruit and lemon, makes an excellent alternative to a traditional farmhouse fruit cake. It keeps well in a cool place.

250g (8oz) courgettes (zucchini), grated
185g (6oz/1¼ cups) mixed dried fruit
125g (4oz/⅓ cup) lemon marmalade
grated rind and juice of 1 lemon
125g (4oz) butter, softened
125g (4oz/¾ cup) light soft brown sugar
2 eggs, beaten
250g (8oz/2 cups) self-raising wholemeal flour
TO DECORATE:
icing sugar for dusting
2 teaspoons lemon rind shreds

1 Lightly grease and line a 20cm (8 inch) round cake tin. Preheat oven to 160C (325F/Gas 3).
2 Put courgettes (zucchini), dried fruit, marmalade, lemon rind and juice into a bowl. Stir until evenly blended. Beat butter and sugar together in a mixing bowl until light and fluffy. Add eggs and beat until thoroughly blended. Stir in courgette (zucchini) mixture, then carefully fold in flour using a spatula until evenly incorporated.
3 Spoon mixture into prepared tin, smooth top and bake for 1 hour, or until cake springs back when lightly pressed in the centre. Cool in tin for 5 minutes, then turn out onto a wire rack, remove paper and invert cake. Leave until cold.
4 To decorate, dredge icing sugar liberally over the top of the cake and sprinkle lemon shreds in the centre.
Serves 16-18.

Date & Apple Cider Loaf

Apples, dates and sultanas are soaked in cider to give a flavoursome tea loaf. Try using other dried fruits – such as peaches, prunes and raisins. You can always vary the spices too.

*185g (6oz/1¼ cups) dried apple
  slices, chopped*
*125g (4oz/¾ cup) dried dates,
  chopped*
125g (4oz/¾ cup) sultanas
250ml (8 fl oz/1 cup) cider
90g (3oz) softened butter
*90g (3oz/½ cup) light soft
  brown sugar*

2 eggs, beaten
*250g (8oz/1¾ cups) granary
  flour*
2 teaspoons baking powder
1 teaspoon ground cloves
TOPPING:
2 tablespoons clear honey
4 pitted dates, chopped
4 dried apple rings, chopped

1 Lightly grease and line a 1kg (2lb) loaf tin. Preheat oven to 160C (325F/Gas 3).

2 Put apples, dates and sultanas in a bowl. Heat cider in a small saucepan, pour onto fruit, stir well, cover with cling film and leave until cold.

3 Beat butter and sugar together in a mixing bowl until light and fluffy. Gradually add eggs, beating well after each addition.

4 Add fruit mixture and stir until evenly blended, then sift in flour, baking powder and cloves. Fold in carefully using a spatula until evenly incorporated.

5 Turn into prepared tin, smooth top and bake in oven for 1 hour 5 minutes to 1 hour 10 minutes, or until cake springs back when pressed in centre. Turn cake out onto a wire rack, remove paper, invert cake and leave until cold.

6 For the topping, place honey in a small saucepan, slowly bring to the boil, then remove from heat. Brush honey over top of cake to glaze. Decorate with date and apple pieces. Brush fruit with more honey glaze. *Serves 16-18.*

Pecan & Pumpkin Cake

Make use of pumpkins when they are around at Hallowe'en. Teamed with pecan nuts and the subtle flavour of mace, they make an interesting cake. Use other nuts for a change, such as brazils, hazelnuts, pine nuts or walnuts.

500g (1lb) pumpkin
125g (4oz) soft margarine
125g (4oz/½ cup) caster sugar
2 tablespoons clear honey
2 eggs, beaten
90g (3oz/½ cup) pecan nuts, chopped
250g (8oz/2 cups) self-raising flour

1 teaspoon ground cinnamon
TOPPING:
2 tablespoons clear honey
¼ teaspoon ground cinnamon
8-12 pecan nuts
2 tablespoons pumpkin seeds

1 Lightly grease and line an 18cm (7 inch) round cake tin. Preheat oven to 160C (325F/Gas 3).
2 Peel pumpkin, chop roughly and cook in 155ml (5 fl oz/ ⅔ cup) boiling water for 2-3 minutes until tender; drain well and mash.
3 Beat margarine, sugar and honey together in a mixing bowl until light and fluffy. Gradually add eggs, beating well after each addition. Stir in pumpkin and nuts. Sift flour and cinnamon together over mixture, then carefully fold in using a spatula.
4 Place mixture in prepared tin, smooth top and bake in oven for 1 hour 10 minutes to 1 hour 15 minutes, or until cake springs back when pressed in the centre. Cool in tin for 5 minutes, turn out onto a wire rack, remove paper, invert cake and leave until cold.
5 For the topping heat honey and cinnamon in a small pan, bring to the boil, then remove from heat. Brush top of cake with glaze and decorate with pecan nuts and pumpkin seeds. Brush nuts and seeds with more glaze. *Serves 20.*

Oatie Banana Bread

A light textured tea loaf made with medium oatmeal, bananas and treacle. You can always use syrup or honey instead of treacle, and vary the nuts if you like.

220g (7oz/1¾ cups) self-
raising flour
1 teaspoon baking powder
90g (3oz/⅔ cup) medium
oatmeal
60g (2oz/⅓ cup) dark soft
brown sugar
125g (4oz) soft margarine
90g (3oz/¼ cup) black treacle

60g (2oz/⅔ cup) walnuts,
chopped
2 bananas, mashed
1 egg
6 tablespoons milk
TOPPING:
1 tablespoon black treacle,
melted
16 dried banana slices
8 walnut halves

1 Lightly grease and line a 1kg (2lb) loaf tin. Preheat oven to 160C (325F/Gas 3).

2 Sift flour and baking powder into a large mixing bowl, add oatmeal, sugar, margarine, black treacle, walnuts, bananas, egg and milk. Mix together with a wooden spoon, then beat for 1-2 minutes until smooth and glossy.

3 Place mixture in prepared tin, smooth top and bake in oven for 1 hour 15 minutes to 1 hour 20 minutes, or until cake springs back when lightly pressed in the centre. Turn out onto a wire rack, remove paper, invert cake and leave until cold.

4 Brush top of cake with warm treacle and decorate with banana slices and walnuts. *Serves 16-18.*

Honey Nut Cake

A lovely mixture of nuts and honey makes a rich moist cake. Choose any combination of nuts: brazils, pecans, pine nuts, hazelnuts, walnuts and almonds are all suitable.

185g (6oz/½ cup) clear honey
2 tablespoons treacle
140ml (4½ fl oz/½ cup)
   sunflower oil
125g (4oz/¾ cup) light soft
   brown sugar
125ml (4 fl oz/½ cup) milk
185g (6oz/1½ cups) plain flour
60g (2oz/½ cup) medium
   oatmeal

125g (4oz/¾ cup) mixed
   chopped nuts
1 egg, beaten
½ teaspoon bicarbonate of soda
TOPPING:
60g (2oz/½ cup) mixed
   chopped nuts
4 tablespoons clear honey

1 Lightly grease and line an 18cm (7 inch) square cake tin. Preheat oven to 160C (325F/Gas 3).
2 Carefully measure honey and treacle into a saucepan, then add oil, sugar and milk. Heat gently, stirring occasionally, until sugar has dissolved. Cool.
3 Meanwhile sift flour into a mixing bowl, add oatmeal, nuts and egg. Add bicarbonate of soda to honey mixture, then pour onto flour mixture and beat with a wooden spoon until smooth.
4 Pour mixture into prepared tin and bake in oven for 1 hour to 1 hour 10 minutes, or until cake springs back when pressed in the centre. Cool in tin for 10 minutes, then turn out onto a wire rack, remove paper and invert cake.
5 For the topping, heat honey in a small pan slowly to the boil, then boil for 1 minute. Add nuts, then pour on top of cake, spreading quickly to cover top evenly. Leave to set.
Serves 20.

Danish Plum Cake

A plain cake with a moist, spiced fruit centre. In place of plums, try greengages, damsons, cherries, apples or pears. Ground mace, all-spice or nutmeg can be used as an alternative to cinnamon. With its fresh fruit topping and filling, this cake should be stored in a cool place and eaten within 2 days.

125g (4oz) butter, softened
125g (4oz/½ cup) caster sugar
1 egg
250g (8oz/2 cups) self-raising
  flour
3 tablespoons milk
FILLING:
375g (12oz) plums, sliced

3 teaspoons caster sugar
1 teaspoon ground cinnamon
TOPPING:
4 plums, sliced
1 tablespoon plum jam, melted
TO FINISH:
icing sugar and ground
  cinnamon for dusting

1 Lightly grease and flour an 18cm (7 inch) ring tin. Preheat oven to 180C (350F/Gas 4).

2 Beat butter and sugar together in a bowl, add egg and beat thoroughly. Fold in flour and milk carefully using a spatula until all flour is incorporated.

3 Spoon half of the mixture into prepared tin and smooth the surface. Arrange plum slices over the mixture and sprinkle evenly with sugar and cinnamon. Cover with remaining mixture and smooth the surface.

4 Bake in oven for 1 hour to 1 hour 10 minutes, or until the cake springs back when pressed in the centre. Loosen edges with a knife, turn out onto a wire rack and leave to cool.

5 For the topping, arrange remaining plum slices around top of cake and brush with melted jam. Dust cake completely with icing sugar sifted with cinnamon. *Serves 16.*

Harvest Cake

A moist, wholesome cake to make when autumnal fruit and nuts are plentiful. It is ideal for keeping or freezing in portions – if you omit the fruit topping and simply glaze with honey.

375g (12oz) plums, stoned and chopped
500g (1lb) pears, peeled and grated
375g (12oz/2 cups) raisins
125g (4oz/¾ cup) hazelnuts, chopped
315g (10 fl oz/1¼ cups) apple juice, warmed
375g (12oz) soft margarine
375g (12oz/2 cups) light soft brown sugar
4 eggs, beaten

500g (1lb/4 cups) self-raising wholewheat flour
2 teaspoons ground mixed spice
8 wheat biscuits (eg Weetabix), total weight 185g (6oz), crumbled
TOPPING:
60ml (2 fl oz/¼ cup) clear honey
4 wheat biscuits (eg Weetabix), total weight 90g (3oz), crumbled
4 red plums, chopped
2 pears, chopped
icing sugar for dusting

1 Lightly grease and line a 30 x 23cm (12 x 9 inch) oblong cake tin or roasting tin. Preheat oven to 160C (325F/Gas 3).
2 Place plums, pears, raisins, hazelnuts and warmed apple juice in a large mixing bowl. Stir well, cover and leave for several hours or overnight.
3 Place margarine, sugar, eggs, flour and spice in another bowl, mix together with a wooden spoon, then beat until light and fluffy.
4 Add wheat biscuits to fruit and mix together, then add the cake mixture and stir until evenly mixed.
5 Spoon mixture into prepared tin and smooth top. Bake in oven for 2½-3 hours, or until cake springs back when pressed in the centre. Leave cake in tin until cold, then turn out, remove paper and invert cake.
6 To make topping, place honey in a saucepan and bring slowly to the boil. Crumble in wheat biscuits and stir in the fruit. Spread mixture over top of cake and leave to cool. Dredge with icing sugar to serve. *Serves 48.*

Strawberry Angel Cake

A light cake made with rice flour and egg whites. Rose water gives it a distinctive flavour. Use any fruits in season, especially raspberries, cherries or redcurrants.

*125g (4oz/1 cup) self-raising
   flour
60g (2oz/⅓ cup) rice flour
125g (4oz/½ cup) caster sugar
1 tablespoon rose water
90ml (3 fl oz/⅓ cup) sunflower
   oil
90ml (3 fl oz/⅓ cup) hot water*

*4 egg whites
FILLING AND TOPPING:
155ml (5 fl oz/⅔ cup) whipping
   cream
3 tablespoons strawberry jam,
   boiled and sieved
250g (8oz) strawberries, sliced*

1 Lightly grease and base line a 19cm (7½ inch) angel cake mould. Preheat oven to 160C (325F/Gas 3).

2 Sift flour and rice flour into a bowl, then stir in sugar. In another bowl, mix together rose water, oil and hot water, then stir into flour. Using a wooden spoon, beat until smooth. Whisk egg whites until stiff, then gradually fold into cake mixture using a spatula until evenly incorporated.

3 Pour mixture into prepared tin, bake in oven for 25-30 minutes, or until cake springs back when lightly pressed in the centre. Loosen edges with a palette knife, turn out onto a wire rack and remove paper. Leave until cold.

4 To make filling, whip cream with 1 tablespoon jam until thick. Reserve 3 tablespoons cream; fold half the strawberry slices into the remainder. Cut cake into 2 layers and sandwich together with strawberry cream filling.

5 Brush top of cake with a little jam. Arrange strawberry slices over top and brush with remaining jam. Spoon or pipe reserved cream in centre and decorate with strawberry slices. *Serves 10.*

NOTE: If you do not have an angel cake mould, use an 18cm (7 inch) round cake tin instead.

St. Clements Drizzle Cake

A delicious sponge cake – soaked in lemon syrup and topped with white chocolate and orange segments. As a variation, try a lemon flavoured sponge soaked in lime and covered with a dark chocolate topping.

1 orange
2 lemons
185g (6oz/1½ cups) self-raising
flour
185g (6oz/¾ cup) caster sugar
185g (6oz) soft margarine
3 eggs, beaten

SYRUP:
125g (4oz/½ cup) caster sugar
TOPPING:
90g (3oz) white chocolate,
melted
orange rind shreds

1 Lightly grease and line a 1kg (2lb) loaf tin. Preheat oven to 160C (325F/Gas 3).

2 Finely grate rind from the orange and 1 lemon. Place in a bowl with flour, sugar, margarine and eggs. Mix together with a wooden spoon, then beat for 1-2 minutes until light and fluffy.

3 Spoon mixture into prepared tin, smooth top and bake for 1¼-1½ hours, or until cake springs back when lightly pressed in the centre. Turn out onto a wire rack, remove paper and allow to cool.

4 To make syrup, squeeze juice from lemons and place in a small pan with sugar. Heat gently, stirring occasionally, until sugar has dissolved, then bring to the boil and boil for 15 seconds. Return cake to tin, pour over syrup and leave until cold.

5 Using a sharp knife, cut pith away from orange and cut out segments; dry on kitchen paper.

6 For the topping, pour white chocolate along top of cake and arrange orange segments overlapping down the centre. Decorate with orange rind shreds. Leave until chocolate is set. *Serves 12.*

Mocha Hazelnut Cake

A light hazelnut cake with a subtle coffee flavour, enhanced by a creamy yogurt filling and a mocha topping.

1 tablespoon coffee granules
3 tablespoons boiling water
185g (6oz) butter, softened
185g (6oz/³/₄ cup) caster sugar
2 eggs, beaten
185g (6oz/1¹/₂ cups) self-raising
 wholemeal flour
2 teaspoons baking powder
125g (4oz/1 cup) hazelnuts,
 toasted and chopped

FILLING:
155ml (5 fl oz/²/₃ cup) double
 (thick) cream
2 tablespoons Greek yogurt
TOPPING:
125g (4oz) plain (dark)
 chocolate, in pieces
1 teaspoon coffee granules
1 tablespoon boiling water
1 tablespoon Greek yogurt
12 hazelnuts

1 Lightly grease and base line two 20cm (8 inch) sandwich tins. Preheat oven to 160C (325G/Gas 3).

2 Dissolve coffee in boiling water. Beat butter and sugar together in a mixing bowl until light and fluffy. Add eggs gradually, beating well after each addition. Sift flour and baking powder onto mixture, add coffee and hazelnuts and fold in carefully using a spatula.

3 Divide mixture between prepared tins, smooth tops and bake in oven for 30-35 minutes, or until cakes spring back when lightly pressed in the centre. Turn out onto a wire rack, remove paper and invert cakes. Leave until cold.

4 To make filling, whip cream with yogurt until thick. Place one third in a piping bag fitted with a star nozzle.

5 To make topping, melt chocolate in a bowl over hot water. Dissolve coffee in boiling water; cool. Stir coffee and yogurt into chocolate until smooth. Spread one third over the base cake and cover with the cream filling. Position other cake on top.

6 Cover top with remaining chocolate and pipe 12 swirls of cream around edge. Place a hazelnut on each swirl of cream. Leave to set. *Serves 12.*

Cranberry & Clementine Cake

A cake with a festive feel, which can be made at any time with cranberries from the freezer.

185g (6oz/1½ cups) self-
  raising flour
185g (6oz/¾ cup) caster sugar
185g (6oz) butter, softened
3 eggs, beaten
60g (2oz/¼ cup) cranberries,
  chopped

FROSTING:
1 clementine
185g (6oz/1 cup) icing sugar,
  sifted
90g (3oz) butter, softened
TO FINISH:
2 tablespoons boiling water
1 tablespoon caster sugar
8 cranberries

1 Lightly grease and line two 20cm (8 inch) round sandwich tins. Preheat oven to 160C (325F/Gas 3).

2 Mix together flour, sugar, butter and eggs in a bowl, then beat with a wooden spoon for 1-2 minutes until smooth and glossy. Stir in cranberries.

3 Divide mixture between prepared tins, smooth tops and bake in oven for 35-40 minutes, or until cakes spring back when lightly pressed in centre. Loosen edge with a palette knife, turn out onto a wire rack and leave until cold.

4 To make frosting, set aside several thin strips of clementine peel. Grate remaining rind finely, squeeze 3 teaspoons juice and place in a bowl with icing sugar and butter. Beat until light and fluffy. Place 4 tablespoons frosting in a piping bag fitted with a small star nozzle.

5 Sandwich cakes together with half the frosting and spread remainder over top. Pipe a frosting lattice and border on top of cake.

6 Cut diamonds from reserved clementine peel. Heat water and sugar in small saucepan, add diamonds and simmer for 30 seconds, then remove with a fork. Add remaining cranberries to syrup and cook gently for 30 seconds. Leave until cold. Decorate top of cake with clementine diamonds and cranberries. *Serves 12.*

Mango & Lime Cake

An unusual but refreshing combination of flavours – the tang of limes with the scented sweetness of mango. Try using paw-paw, guavas or pineapple in place of mango for other tropical flavours.

125g (4oz/½ cup) caster sugar
4 eggs
125g (4oz/1 cup) self-raising
flour
grated rind of 1 lime
60g (2oz) butter, melted

FILLING:
125g (4oz/½ cup) soft cheese
125ml (4 fl oz/½ cup) fromage
frais or Greek yogurt
2 teaspoons clear honey
1 mango, diced
2 lime slices, in sections

1 Lightly grease and line a 33 x 23cm (13 x 9 inch) Swiss roll tin. Preheat oven to 180C (350F/Gas 4).

2 Place sugar and eggs in a heatproof bowl over a saucepan of simmering water and whisk until pale and thick. Remove bowl from saucepan and whisk until the mixture leaves a trail when the beaters are lifted.

3 Sift flour over surface of mixture, add lime rind and butter. Fold in carefully using a spatula until all the flour and butter are incorporated. Pour mixture into prepared tin and tilt tin from side to side to level mixture. Bake in oven for 15-20 minutes, or until cake springs back when lightly pressed in the centre.

4 Turn out on a wire rack, carefully remove paper, invert cake and leave until cold.

5 To make filling, in a bowl beat together soft cheese, fromage frais or yogurt and honey until smooth. Set aside one third of the cheese mixture. Stir two thirds of the mango into remaining filling.

6 Cut cake across width into 3 equal pieces and sandwich together with mango filling. Spread reserved cheese mixture evenly over top of cake and sprinkle centre with diced mango. Decorate edges with lime slices. *Serves 12.*

Birthday Cake

A light, moist fruit cake suitable for icing or leaving plain. Once iced, it will keep up to 3 months and may be decorated for any occasion. For the cake shown opposite you will need fresh flowers and about 2 metres of fancy ribbon.

500g (1lb/3 cups) mixed
  dried fruit
125g (4oz/³/4 cup) glacé cherries,
  chopped
60g (2oz/¹/2 cup) flaked almonds
grated rind and juice of
  1 small orange
375g (12oz/3 cups) plain flour
1 teaspoon ground mixed spice
280g (9oz/1¹/2 cups) light soft
  brown sugar

280g (9oz) butter, softened
4 eggs, beaten
ICING AND DECORATION:
750g (1lb 8oz) white marzipan
3 tablespoons apricot jam,
  boiled and sieved
750g (1lb 8oz) ready-to-
  roll icing
cornflour for dusting

1 Prepare an 18cm (7 inch) square cake tin as for Simnel Cake (page 52). Preheat oven to 140C (275F/Gas 1).
2 In a bowl, mix together dried fruit, cherries, almonds, orange rind and juice. Place remaining cake ingredients in another bowl, mix together with a wooden spoon, then beat for 1-2 minutes until smooth and glossy. Add fruit mixture and stir well.
3 Place mixture in prepared tin, smooth top and bake in oven for 1³/4-2 hours, or until a warm skewer inserted in the centre comes out clean. Cool in tin, turn out, remove paper and place on a 20cm (8 inch) square cake board.
4 Roll out marzipan to a 23cm (10 inch) square. Brush cake with apricot glaze, cover with marzipan and trim off excess to neaten. Roll out icing on a surface lightly sprinkled with cornflour to a 23cm (10 inch) square. Place on cake, smooth top and sides, and trim off excess to neaten base.
5 Crimp top and base of cake using a small crimping tool dipped in cornflour. Tie ribbon around side of cake and arrange flowers on top. *Serves 24-30.*

Simnel Cake

A traditional cake at Easter time. In my version tiny balls of marzipan are scattered throughout the moist, light fruit cake, instead of the usual solid marzipan layer.

375g (12oz/2 cups) mixed
   dried fruit
50g (2oz/⅓ cup) glacé cherries
grated rind and juice of
   1 small lemon
185g (6oz) margarine
185g (6oz/1 cup) light soft
   brown sugar
250g (8oz/2 cups) self-raising
   wholewheat flour

3 eggs, beaten
375g (12oz) yellow marzipan
TOPPING:
2 tablespoons apricot jam,
   boiled and sieved
2 tablespoons icing sugar, sifted
2 teaspoons lemon juice
TO DECORATE:
sugar-coated chocolate eggs

1 Lightly grease and line an 18cm (7 inch) round cake tin with greaseproof paper. Tie a double thickness band of brown paper around the outside of the tin and sit on a baking tray lined with a double thickness of brown paper. Preheat oven to 150C (300F/Gas 2).

2 In a bowl, mix together dried fruit, cherries, lemon rind and juice. Place margarine, sugar, flour and eggs in a mixing bowl. Mix together with a wooden spoon, then beat for 1-2 minutes until smooth and glossy. Stir in fruit.

3 Shape 125g (4oz) marzipan into small balls. Spoon cake mixture into prepared tin and distribute marzipan balls evenly throughout mixture. Smooth the surface. Bake in oven for 2½-2¾ hours, or until a warm skewer inserted into the centre of the cake comes out clean. Cool in tin. Turn out and remove paper.

4 Brush top of cake with apricot glaze. Shape 11 tiny marzipan eggs; roll remainder into an 18 cm (7 inch) round and position on cake; flute edge. Arrange marzipan eggs on top. Place under a preheated grill to brown lightly.

5 Mix icing sugar with lemon juice and spread in centre of cake. Top with eggs and leave to set. *Serves 12.*

Christmas Cake

A rich, easy-to-cut celebration fruit cake. Wrapped in foil, it will store in a cool place for up to 3 months.

750g (1lb 8oz/4½ cups) mixed
  dried fruit
125g (4oz/¾ cup) glacé
  cherries, chopped
125g (4oz/1 cup) dried
  apricots, chopped
90g (3oz/½ cup) stoned
  prunes, chopped
60g (2oz/⅔ cup) brazil
  nuts, chopped
grated rind and juice of 1 lemon
3 tablespoons brandy
280g (9oz/2¼ cups) plain flour
2 teaspoons ground mixed spice
220g (7oz) butter, softened

60g (2oz/½ cup) ground
  almonds
220g (7oz/1⅓ cups) dark soft
  brown sugar
1½ tablespoons black treacle
4 eggs, beaten
ICING AND DECORATION:
750g (1lb 8oz) white marzipan
3 tablespoons apricot jam,
  boiled and sieved
2 egg whites
2 teaspoons glycerine
1 teaspoon lemon juice
500g (1lb/3 cups) icing
  sugar, sifted

1 Prepare a 20cm (8 inch) round cake tin as for Simnel Cake (page 52). Preheat oven to 140C (275F/Gas 1).

2 In a bowl, mix together dried fruit, cherries, apricots, prunes, nuts, lemon rind, juice and brandy.

3 Mix remaining cake ingredients in a large bowl, then beat with a wooden spoon for 1-2 minutes until smooth and glossy. Add fruit mixture and stir well.

4 Place mixture in prepared tin, smooth top and bake in oven for 3-3¼ hours, or until a warm skewer inserted into centre of cake comes out clean. Cool in tin. Turn out, remove paper and place on a 25cm (10 inch) cake board.

5 Roll out marzipan to a 25cm (10 inch) round. Brush cake with apricot glaze, cover with marzipan and trim.

6 Place egg whites, glycerine and lemon juice in a bowl. Gradually beat in icing sugar until icing peaks softly. Spread evenly over cake. Press a small palette knife onto icing and pull away sharply to form peaks, leaving a band for ribbon. Apply ribbon and decorations. *Serves 24-30.*

Praline Gâteau

4 eggs
125g (4oz/½ cup) caster sugar
100g (3½oz/⅞ cup) self-raising
  flour, sifted
15g (½oz/2 tablespoons) cocoa
  powder
CRÈME AU BEURRE:
155ml (5 fl oz/⅔ cup) water

140g (4½oz/½ cup + 3 tea-
  spoons) caster sugar
3 egg yolks
235g (7½oz) unsalted butter
PRALINE:
125g (4oz/½ cup) caster sugar
4 tablespoons water
90g (3oz/½ cup) hazelnuts

1 Lightly grease, base line and flour two 18cm (7 inch) shallow square tins. Preheat oven to 180C (350F/Gas 4).

2 Place eggs and sugar in a heatproof bowl over a saucepan of simmering water and whisk until mixture becomes thick and pale. Remove bowl from pan and whisk until mixture leaves a trail on the surface when beaters are lifted.

3 Pour half the mixture into another bowl and fold in 60g (2oz/½ cup) sifted flour. Fold remaining flour and cocoa into other half. Pour each into a prepared tin and bake in oven for 20-25 minutes, or until cakes spring back when lightly pressed in centre. Cool on a wire rack.

4 Make crème au beurre as for Summer Lemon Sponge (page 4, step 4). Set aside 5 tablespoons for decoration.

5 To make praline, cover 2 baking sheets with foil and brush with oil. Place water and sugar in saucepan, heat gently until sugar is dissolved, then add hazelnuts and boil rapidly until syrup is golden brown. Remove from heat. Using an oiled spoon, lift out 20 nuts individually and place on 1 baking sheet; drizzle 5 caramel pieces onto same baking sheet; set aside for decoration. Pour remaining nuts and caramel onto second baking sheet. Leave until cold, then crush praline; add half to crème au beurre.

6 Cut each cake into 2 layers. Sandwich the layers with praline crème au beurre; cover top and sides with remainder. Coat sides with remaining praline. Pipe border around edge and decorate with nuts and caramel pieces.
Serves 18.

Coffee Gâteau

3 eggs
90g (3oz/¹/₃ cup) caster sugar
2 teaspoons coffee granules
1 teaspoon boiling water
90g (3oz/³/₄ cup) self-raising
    flour
COFFEE MERINGUE ICING:
2 teaspoons coffee granules
1 teaspoon boiling water

2 egg whites
125g (4oz/³/₄ cup) icing
    sugar, sifted
155g (5oz) unsalted butter,
    softened
TO FINISH:
20 ratafias
chocolate coffee beans

1 Line 3 baking sheets with non-stick baking paper and draw a 20cm (8 inch) circle on each. Preheat oven to 200C (400F/Gas 6).

2 Place eggs and sugar in a heatproof bowl over a saucepan of simmering water and whisk until thick and pale. Remove bowl from saucepan and whisk until mixture leaves a trail on the surface when beaters are lifted. Dissolve coffee granules in water. Sift flour onto surface of mixture, add coffee and carefully fold in.

3 Divide mixture between circles, spread evenly to edges and bake in oven for 10-15 minutes, or until golden brown and springy to touch. Cool on paper, then carefully peel off.

4 To make coffee meringue icing, dissolve coffee granules in water. Whisk egg whites and icing sugar in a heatproof bowl over simmering water until thick and white. Remove bowl from saucepan and whisk until meringue is cool and stands in peaks. Beat butter in a separate bowl until light and fluffy, then gradually whisk in meringue and coffee.

5 Set aside 9 ratafias for decoration; crush remainder. Sandwich layers together with icing, cover sides with more icing and coat with crushed ratafias. Cover top with a thin layer of icing and pipe on a decorative border. Decorate with chocolate coffee beans and ratafias. *Serves 12.*

Chocolate Triangle Gâteau

185g (6oz) plain (dark)
  chocolate, in pieces
125g (4oz) unsalted butter
60ml (2 fl oz/¼ cup) dark rum
60g (2oz/⅓ cup) raisins
3 eggs, separated
125g (4oz/½ cup) caster sugar
125g (4oz/1 cup) plain flour
60g (2oz/½ cup) ground
  almonds

CHOCOLATE ICING:
185g (6oz) plain (dark)
  chocolate, in pieces
90ml (3 fl oz/⅓ cup) milk
FILLING:
155ml (5 fl oz/⅔ cup) double
  (thick) cream, whipped
TO DECORATE:
90g (3oz) white chocolate,
  melted

1 Lightly grease and line an 18cm (7 inch) square cake tin. Preheat oven to 180C (350F/Gas 4).

2 Melt chocolate with butter in bowl over saucepan of hot water. Heat rum and raisins together until almost boiling, then cool. Stir into chocolate mixture.

3 Whisk egg yolks and sugar together until thick and pale. Stir in chocolate mixture. Carefully fold in flour and ground almonds. Whisk egg whites until stiff and fold into mixture until evenly incorporated. Pour into prepared tin, level top and bake in oven for 40-50 minutes, or until cake springs back when lightly pressed in centre. Cool in tin, turn out and remove paper. Cut into 2 layers.

4 To make chocolate icing, melt chocolate with milk; let cool. Fold 1 tablespoon chocolate icing into whipped cream and use a third to sandwich layers together. Spread top and sides with remaining cream to cover evenly. Chill.

5 When chocolate icing is thick enough to coat back of spoon, quickly pour all over cake, spread evenly and leave to set.

6 Spread white chocolate evenly on non-stick baking paper to an 18cm (7 inch) square. Leave until set. Invert chocolate onto another piece of paper, carefully peel off backing paper and cut into triangles. Use to decorate gâteau. *Serves 16.*

Clementine Gâteau

155g (5oz/²⁄₃ cup) caster sugar
155g (5oz/1¼ cups) self-raising
  flour
60g (2oz/¼ cup) brazil
  nuts, ground
5 eggs, separated
60ml (2 fl oz/¼ cup) sunflower
  oil
60ml (2 fl oz/¼ cup) boiling
  water

grated rind of 1 clementine
FILLING AND DECORATION:
315ml (10 fl oz/1¼ cups)
  whipping cream, whipped
3 clementines
30g (1oz/¼ cup) chocolate
  sugar strands
30g (1oz) plain (dark) chocolate,
  melted

1 Lightly grease and base line a 20cm (8 inch) moule à manque tin or round cake tin. Lightly flour sides of tin. Preheat oven to 180C (350F/Gas 4).

2 In a bowl, mix together sugar, flour and nuts. Whisk egg yolks and oil together in a separate bowl, add water and clementine rind, then pour onto dry ingredients and beat until smooth and glossy.

3 Whisk egg whites until stiff and carefully fold into cake mixture. Pour mixture into prepared tin, smooth top and bake for 40-45 minutes, or until cake springs back when lightly pressed in the centre. Turn out onto a wire rack, remove paper and leave until cold. Cut cake into 3 layers.

4 Set aside 5 tablespoons cream for decoration. Fold grated rind of 1 clementine into remaining cream. Cut another clementine into 8 wedges; reserve for decoration. Peel remaining 2 clementines and chop flesh.

5 Sandwich cake layers together with a third of the cream and the chopped fruit. Spread side with cream and coat with chocolate strands. Cover top with remaining cream and pipe a decorative border around edge, using reserved cream.

6 Place melted chocolate in a greaseproof paper piping bag, snip off point and pipe 20 looped designs onto non-stick baking paper. When dry, peel off. Decorate gâteau with clementine wedges and chocolate pieces. *Serves 12.*

Nectarine Melba Roulade

Impressive yet easy-to-make, this walnut sponge roll is filled with a creamy raspberry and nectarine filling and served with a fresh raspberry sauce. You can of course use peaches.

ROULADE:
3 eggs, separated
2 teaspoons water
185g (6oz/³/₄ cup) caster sugar
125g (4oz/1 cup) plain flour
60g (2oz/¹/₂ cup) ground
walnuts

FILLING AND DECORATION:
185g (6oz/³/₄ cup) soft cheese
90ml (3 fl oz/¹/₃ cup) Greek
yogurt
3 nectarines, stoned and sliced
375g (12oz/2 cups) raspberries
2 tablespoons icing sugar

1 Lightly grease and line a 33 x 23 cm (13 x 9 inch) Swiss roll tin with non-stick baking paper. Preheat oven to 200C (400F/Gas 6).

2 Whisk egg whites with water until stiff. Gradually add sugar, whisking well after each addition, until mixture stands in peaks. Beat egg yolks, then fold into meringue. Mix together flour and nuts and carefully fold into meringue.

3 Transfer mixture to prepared tin, level top and bake for 15-20 minutes, or until lightly browned and firm. Invert onto a piece of non-stick paper sprinkled with caster sugar. Trim off edges, then loosely roll up from short edge, enclosing paper. Cool on wire rack.

4 To make filling, beat together soft cheese and yogurt; set aside 3 tablespoons for decoration. Reserve 8 nectarine slices for decoration, chop remainder and add to cheese mixture with 2 tablespoons raspberries. Mix lightly.

5 Carefully unroll cake and remove paper, spread filling evenly over and reroll firmly. Decorate with piped cheese mixture, nectarine slices and 8 raspberries.

6 Sieve remaining raspberries into a bowl and stir in 1 tablespoon icing sugar. Dust roulade with remaining icing sugar and serve with raspberry sauce. *Serves 8.*

Canteloup Gâteau

Fragrant canteloup melon with crystallized ginger and lime makes this gâteau refreshingly different. Galia melon is equally good.

4 eggs
125g (4oz/½ cup) caster sugar
125g (4oz/1 cup) plain flour
60g (2oz) unsalted butter,
   melted
finely grated rind of 1 lime
FILLING:
315ml (10 fl oz/1¼ cups) double
   (thick) cream

4 tablespoons Greek yogurt
finely grated rind of 1 lime
30g (1oz/¼ cup) crystallized
   ginger, chopped
TO DECORATE:
125g (4oz/¾ cup) pistachio nuts
1 canteloup melon
crystallized ginger slices

1 Lightly grease, base line and flour a 23cm (9 inch) spring form cake tin. Preheat oven to 180C (350F/Gas 4).

2 Place eggs and sugar in a heatproof bowl over a saucepan of simmering water and whisk until thick and pale. Remove bowl from saucepan and whisk until mixture leaves a trail on the surface when beaters are lifted.

3 Sift flour onto mixture, add butter and lime rind. Carefully fold in using a spatula until evenly incorporated. Pour mixture into prepared tin and bake for 35-40 minutes, until cake springs back when lightly pressed in centre.

4 Loosen edges of cake with a knife, release tin and carefully turn cake out onto a wire rack. Leave until cold, then cut into 3 layers.

5 Whip cream and yogurt together until thick; reserve 6 tablespoons for piping. Set aside one third of remaining cream. Fold lime rind and ginger into the other two thirds; use to sandwich cake layers together. Cover top and sides with remaining cream. Reserve 12 whole pistachio nuts; chop remainder and use to coat sides of cake.

6 Cut melon in half, scoop into small balls using a melon baller and arrange on top of gâteau. Pipe a cream border around the edge and decorate with ginger and pistachio nuts. *Serves 12.*

Cheesecake Gâteau

A cheesecake with a difference – soft sponge and tangy fruity cheese layers. Other soft fruits can be used.

SPONGE BASE:
3 eggs
90g (3oz/²⁄₃ cup) caster sugar
90g (3oz/³⁄₄ cup) plain flour
FILLING:
185g (6oz/1¹⁄₂ cups) redcurrants
185g (6oz/1¹⁄₂ cups)
  blackcurrants
2 tablespoons caster sugar

1¹⁄₂ packets lemon flavour jelly
125g (4oz) unsalted butter
250g (8oz/1 cup) soft cheese
155ml (5 fl oz/²⁄₃ cup)
  natural yogurt
TO FINISH:
155ml (5 fl oz/²⁄₃ cup) whipping
  cream, whipped
red and blackcurrants

1 Lightly grease and line a 33 x 23 cm (13 x 9 inch) Swiss roll tin. Preheat oven to 180C (350F/Gas 4).

2 Place eggs and sugar in a heatproof bowl over a pan of simmering water. Whisk until thick and pale. Remove bowl from pan and whisk until mixture leaves a trail on surface when beaters are lifted. Sift flour over mixture and fold in carefully. Pour mixture into prepared tin. Bake in oven for 10-15 minutes. Cool in tin.

3 Place fruit in separate pans; add 1 tablespoon water to each pan. Bring to boil, remove from heat and sieve into separate bowls; into each stir 1 tablespoon sugar.

4 Gently heat jelly and butter in a saucepan until melted. Put soft cheese, yogurt and jelly mixture into a food processor or blender and process until smooth. Divide between fruit mixtures, stirring well. Leave until thickened.

5 Spread blackcurrant mixture over sponge base in tin; chill to set quickly. Spread redcurrant mixture on top and leave for several hours or overnight until set.

6 Carefully invert cake onto a baking sheet lined with non-stick paper. Peel off lining paper and turn cake right way up. Cut into three 10 cm (4 inch) strips. Sandwich layers together with cream. Decorate gâteau with piped cream and fresh fruit. *Serves 8.*

Strawberry Cream Torte

Thin crispy layers filled with pastry cream and fruit make a light summer gâteau. Choose any fruits in season.

TORTE:
2 egg whites
125g (4oz/³⁄₄ cup) icing sugar, sifted
60g (2oz/¹⁄₂ cup) plain flour
60g (2oz) unsalted butter, melted
2 tablespoons chopped pine nuts
60g (2oz) chocolate, grated
PASTRY CREAM:
155ml (5 fl oz/²⁄₃ cup) milk

15g (¹⁄₂oz/6 teaspoons) plain flour
2 teaspoons caster sugar
1 egg yolk
1 teaspoon vanilla essence
155ml (5 fl oz/²⁄₃ cup) double (thick) cream, whipped
TO FINISH:
250g (8oz/1¹⁄₂ cups) strawberries, sliced
icing sugar for dusting

1 Line 3 baking sheets with non-stick baking paper. Draw on three 18cm (7 inch) circles and eight 7.5cm (3 inch) circles. Preheat oven to 200C (400F/Gas 6).

2 Whisk egg whites until very stiff. Gradually whisk in icing sugar. Add flour and butter; whisk until smooth. Spread a teaspoonful of mixture in each small circle. Spread remainder over large circles and sprinkle large circles with the nuts and half the grated chocolate.

3 Bake small circles for 5-8 minutes, remove with a palette knife and fold each into a cone shape. Wedge in wire rack to cool. Cook large circles for 10-12 minutes. Cool on paper.

4 To make pastry cream, whisk 1 tablespoon milk with the flour, sugar, egg yolk and vanilla essence in a bowl. Bring remaining milk to the boil. Add to the flour mixture, whisking thoroughly. Return to saucepan, bring to the boil and cook, stirring, for 1 minute. Leave until cold, then fold into cream.

5 Set aside a quarter of pastry cream. Add rest of chocolate and two thirds of strawberry slices to remaining pastry cream and use to sandwich torte layers together. Pipe cones with pastry cream and arrange on torte. Dust with icing sugar and decorate with strawberry slices. *Serves 8.*

Fruit Choux Gâteau

SHORTBREAD BASE:
90g (3oz/¾ cup) plain flour
30g (1oz/5 teaspoons) caster
 sugar
60g (2oz) unsalted butter
CHOUX PASTRY:
155ml (5 fl oz/⅔ cup) water
60g (2oz) butter
75g (2½oz/⅔ cup) plain flour
2 eggs, beaten
PASTRY CREAM:
155ml (5 fl oz/⅔ cup) milk

15g (½oz/6 teaspoons) plain
 flour
2 teaspoons caster sugar
1 egg yolk
1 teaspoon vanilla essence
155ml (5 fl oz/⅔ cup) double
 (thick cream), whipped
TO FINISH:
2 tablespoons apricot jam
6 apricots, sliced
125g (4oz) seedless grapes
icing sugar for dusting

1 To make shortbread base, sift flour and sugar into a bowl, rub in butter until mixture begins to bind together, then knead into a ball. Roll out on a lightly floured surface to a 20cm (8 inch) round. Place on a large floured baking sheet and prick base. Chill. Preheat oven to 200C (400F/Gas 6).

2 To make choux pastry, place water and butter in saucepan, heat gently until butter has melted, then bring to boil. Add flour all at once, beating vigorously with a wooden spoon until mixture forms a ball. Gradually add eggs, beating well after each addition.

3 Place choux pastry in piping bag fitted with a 1 cm (½ inch) plain nozzle. Pipe a border of small choux balls around edge of shortbread. Pipe remaining mixture into small balls on baking sheet. Bake shortbread and choux balls in oven for 20-25 minutes, or until well risen and golden brown. Let cool for 10 minutes, then carefully transfer to a wire rack and leave until cold.

4 Make pastry cream as for Strawberry Cream Torte (page 70). Put two thirds into a piping bag. Split each choux bun and pipe in pastry cream.

5 Spread shortbread base with jam and remaining pastry cream. Cover with three quarters of the apricots. Arrange choux buns on top and decorate with remaining apricots and grapes. Dust with icing sugar. Serves 12.

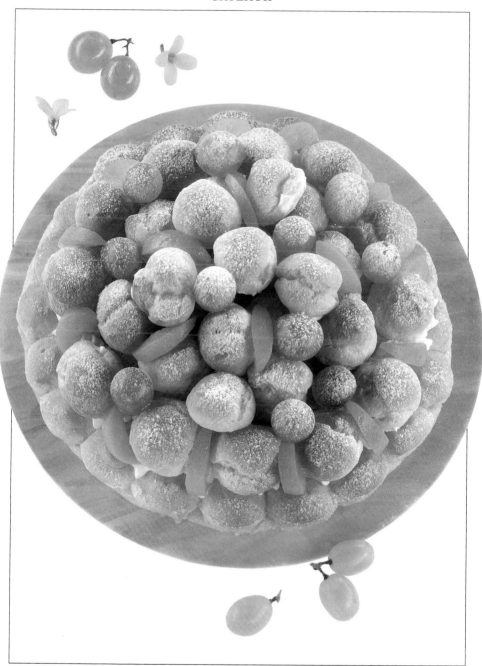

Franzipan Fruit Gâteau

Layers of crisp light puff pastry filled with a moist almond filling and topped with a mixture of fresh fruits in season. Cut the pastry into any shape – square, round, oval or petal-shaped.

375g (12oz) puff pastry, thawed
if frozen
FILLING:
125g (4oz/1¼ cups) ground
almonds
125g (4oz/¾ cup) icing sugar,
sifted
1 teaspoon almond essence
30g (1oz/¼ cup) plain flour

125g (4oz) unsalted butter,
softened
2 eggs, beaten
250g (8oz/2 cups) mixed soft
fruits, eg blueberries,
raspberries, cherries,
redcurrants
icing sugar for dusting

1 Cut pastry in half and roll out each piece on a lightly floured surface to a 25cm (10 inch) round. Place on a floured baking sheet and chill while making filling.

2 Place ground almonds, icing sugar, almond essence and flour in a bowl and stir well. In another bowl, beat butter until soft, stir in almond mixture and eggs, then beat until smooth.

3 Prick 1 pastry layer with a fork, spread almond filling over this layer to within 2.5cm (1 inch) of edge and cover with all but 2 tablespoons of the soft fruits. Dampen pastry edge, cover with remaining pastry round and seal edges well. Using a sharp knife, cut pastry edge into scallops and mark fine lines on the top, radiating from the centre. Chill for 30 minutes before baking.

4 Preheat oven to 220C (425F/Gas 7). Bake pastry for 20 minutes, then reduce oven temperature to 200C (400F/Gas 6) and bake for a further 20 minutes or until pastry is well risen and golden brown. Cool on a wire rack. Dredge surface with icing sugar and place under a preheated hot grill to caramelize. Decorate the centre with the reserved soft fruits. *Serves 12.*

Hazelnut & Redcurrant Gâteau

A melt-in-the-mouth meringue, richly flavoured with hazelnuts and filled with cream and redcurrants. Try any soft fruit in season, such as cherries, raspberries or strawberries, and flavour the meringue with lightly toasted walnuts, pine nuts or almonds.

MERINGUE:
185g (6oz/³⁄4 cup) toasted hazelnuts, finely chopped
1 teaspoon orange flower water
¹⁄2 teaspoon cream of tartar
1 teaspoon cornflour

4 egg whites
250g (8oz/1 cup) caster sugar
FILLING:
185g (6oz/¹⁄2 cup) redcurrants
185ml (5 fl oz/²⁄3 cup) whipping cream, whipped

1 Lightly grease and base line two 20cm (8 inch) sandwich tins with non-stick baking paper. Sprinkle 2 teaspoons hazelnuts onto the sides of the tins and shake to coat evenly. Preheat oven to 180C (350F/Gas 4).
2 In a small bowl, mix together orange flower water, cream of tartar and cornflour. Whisk egg whites until stiff. Gradually add sugar, whisking well after each addition. Whisk in cornflour mixture until meringue is stiff and glossy. Carefully fold in 125g (4oz/¹⁄2 cup) hazelnuts, using a spatula, until evenly incorporated.
3 Divide mixture between prepared tins, smooth tops and bake in oven for 45-50 minutes until meringue is crisp and lightly browned on surface, but soft in centre. Cool in tin. Carefully turn out meringues and remove paper.
4 To make filling, fold three quarters of the redcurrants into half of the cream and use to sandwich the meringue layers together. Cover the sides with a thin layer of cream and coat evenly with the remaining chopped hazelnuts. Put the remaining cream in a piping bag fitted with a star nozzle and pipe a ring in the middle and a shell border around the edge. Fill the centre with the remaining redcurrants.
Serves 10.

Summer Fruit Meringue Basket

MERINGUE:
6 egg whites
¾ teaspoon cream of tartar
470g (15oz/2¼ cups) caster
  sugar
FILLING:
625g (20 fl oz/2½ cups)
  whipping cream, whipped

45g (1½ oz/⅓ cup) amaretti
  biscuits, crushed
2 tablespoons Marsala
625g (1lb/3 cups) mixed soft
  fruits, eg cherries,
  strawberries, raspberries,
  redcurrants

1 Line 3 baking sheets with non-stick baking paper; draw a 20 x 15cm (8 x 6 inch) oval on each. Preheat oven to 110C (225F/Gas ¼).
2 Whisk 4 egg whites and ½ teaspoon cream of tartar in a bowl until very stiff. Gradually whisk in 315g (10oz/ 1¼ cups) sugar, until meringue stands in stiff peaks. Place in a large piping bag fitted with a 1cm (½ inch) plain nozzle.
3 Pipe oval rings on each baking sheet. Fill one of these with piped meringue to form the basket base. Pipe a second oval ring on edge of base. Place all 3 baking sheets in oven for 20-30 minutes, or until meringue is firm and white.
4 Loosen oval rings from paper and secure one on top of the other on edge of basket base, with a little meringue. Spread remaining meringue around sides of basket. Bake for another 20-30 minutes.
5 Make up second batch of meringue using remaining egg whites, cream of tartar and sugar as before. Pipe a basket weave pattern around basket. Pipe 2 handles on a lined baking sheet. Bake basket and handles for 45 minutes to 1 hour until crisp and white. Cool on paper.
6 Sandwich handles together with cream. Fold amaretti biscuits, Marsala and half the soft fruit into remaining cream and use to fill basket. Secure handles in position and decorate basket with remaining fruit, ribbons and flowers.
Serves 10.

Index